Dedication

This book is mainly dedicated to my family.
To my very supportive husband and best friend, Kirkland:
Thank you for always reminding me to believe in my gifts.
I appreciate you and will always love you.
I'm forever grateful that you are a person who always honors your promises.
Thank you for being an integral part of our experiences within other cultures.

To my children, De'Angelo, Ari'el, Landon, and Amara:
I encourage you to believe in yourselves and to work smart to be an
enlightening source to the world.
Continue to stay focused and be honorable.
Thank you, especially to Amara, for allowing me to share some of your cultural
experiences and journeys through this book.

It is also dedicated to anyone who is of various descents or cultures.
Love all of yourself and take time to learn about your cultural connections.

For inquiries, contact sabrinahenry1977@gmail.com
www.amazon.com/author/sabrinahenry

Names: Henry, Sabrina N., author / Riani, Lidya, illustrator
Title: Colorful Cultures of Me / written by Sabrina N. Henry; illustrated by Lidya Riani
Summary: In this book, Amara shares her connection to her three cultures and three countries
Subjects: Cultures, Family, Jamaica, Traveling, United Arab Emirates, U.S.A.

Printed in U.S.A.

The Colorful Cultures of Me

Sharing my connections to the United Arab Emirates, Jamaica, and U.S.A

Written by
Sabrina N. Henry

Illustrated by
Lidya Riani

A Little About Me...

Hi! I am Amara.
I am from several different cultures.
My parents and family are helping me
to learn about myself and where I am
from. I would like to share with you
some cool information about my
different backgrounds. I will help you
to learn a little more about my
3 countries and their cultures.

How Did I Get Here?

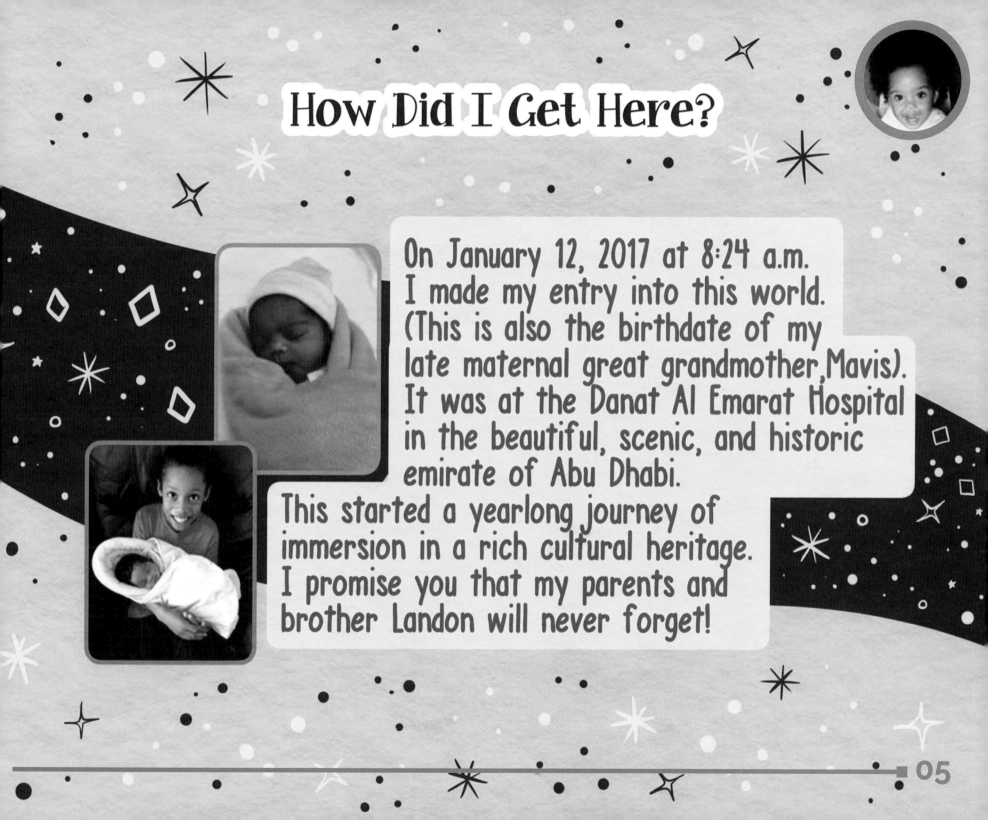

On January 12, 2017 at 8:24 a.m.
I made my entry into this world.
(This is also the birthdate of my
late maternal great grandmother, Mavis).
It was at the Danat Al Emarat Hospital
in the beautiful, scenic, and historic
emirate of Abu Dhabi.
This started a yearlong journey of
immersion in a rich cultural heritage.
I promise you that my parents and
brother Landon will never forget!

A Lot of Firsts

On January 12, 2018, on my 1st birthday, I flew to the U.S.A for the 1st time. I met my eldest brother, my sister, and my paternal grandma and grandpa for the 1st time. Later, I met more family and relatives. A few days after, I flew to Jamaica for the 1st time. There, I met a lot of other family members and got more tastes of the culture too.

Now follow me to learn about the U.A.E.

Welcome to
The United Arab Emirates (U.A.E)

Abu Dhabi

U.A.E

This is the country where I was born.
It is called The United Arab Emirates (U.A.E).
I was born in the capital which is Abu Dhabi.

Where is the United Arab Emirates Located?

The U.A.E is in the Middle East/southwest Asia, bordering the Gulf of Oman and the Persian Gulf, between Oman and Saudi Arabia.

Persian Gulf

Gulf of Oman

United Arab Emirates

Saudi Arabia

Oman

How many emirates are in the United Arab Emirates?

There are 7 emirates in the U.A.E. They are Abu Dhabi, Dubai, Sharjah, Fujairah, Ras al Khaimah, Umm al-Quwain, and Ajman. Abu Dhabi is the capital of the U.A.E.

Ras al-Khaimah

Umm al-Quwain

Ajman

Dubai

Fujairah

5

6

7

4

3

2

Sharjah

Abu Dhabi

1

What is the official currency of the United Arab Emirates?

Personal Specimen

The money used in the U.A.E. is the dirham (AED or Arab Emirate Dirham – also commonly shortened to Dhs or DH). There are 100 fils in a dirham. Notes come in denominations of 5, 10, 20, 50, 100, 200, 500 and 1,000 dirhams.

Personal Specimen

What does the flag of the United Arab Emirates look like?

The colors of the flag of the U.A.E are red, green, white, and black.

The green represents hope and prosperity.
White symbolizes purity, cleanliness, peace, and honesty.
Black is a representation of strength of the mind.
Finally, the red symbolizes the unity among the emirates.

What about the languages spoken in the U.A.E?

English	Arabic
Yes	Na'am
No	La
Thank you	Shukran
Sorry	Aasef
Let's go	Yalla
Milk	Halib

Arabic is the official language of the U.A.E. Although Arabic is the official language there, English is widely spoken and understood. Since the UAE is home to a large expatriate community, several other languages are widely spoken which primarily include Persian, Hindi, Urdu, Bengali, and Mandarin.

What famous landmarks are in the United Arab Emirates?

Sheik Zayed Grand Mosque

The Emirates Palace

Burj Khalifa

Burj Al Arab

Some popular landmarks in the U.A.E are the Sheik Zayed Grand Mosque, the Emirates Palace, Burj Khalifa, and Burj Al Arab. There is a lot more too!

What are some of the things for which the United Arab Emirates is famous?

Palm Jebel Ali

Deira Island

Palm Jumeirah

The U.A.E. is famous for manmade islands, huge skyscrapers and for having the tallest building in the world (the Burj Khalifa in Dubai). Palm Islands are three artificial islands. They are Palm Jumeirah, Deira Island and Palm Jebel Ali, on the coast of Dubai.

What are some popular foods/dishes/cuisines from the United Arab Emirates?

The U.A.E. has a wide variety of popular foods/dishes/cuisines. Biryani, fattoush, shawarma, al harees, hummus, stuffed camel, camel milk and dates are just a few.

Biryani

Fattoush

Shawarma

Al Harees

....more foods/dishes/cuisines from the United Arab Emirates

Hummus

Stuffed Camel

Camel Milk

Dates

It would be cool if you could visit. You would enjoy the scenery, food, and people.

Welcome to
Jamaica

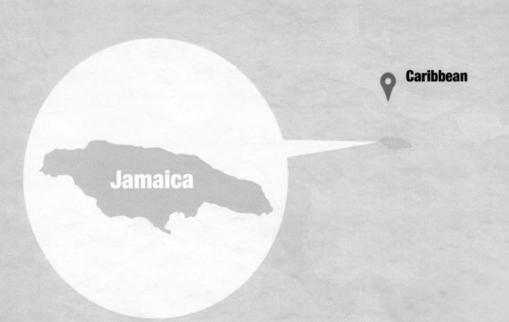

Caribbean

Jamaica

This is the country where my grandparents were born. It is called Jamaica.
My parents and eldest brother were also born here.
It is a small island in the Caribbean.
I will tell you more as you read along.

Where is Jamaica Located?

Jamaica is in the West Indies. This is a set of islands between southeast United States and northern South America. It is surrounded by the Caribbean Sea.

Caribbean Sea

Jamaica

Caribbean Sea

Caribbean Sea

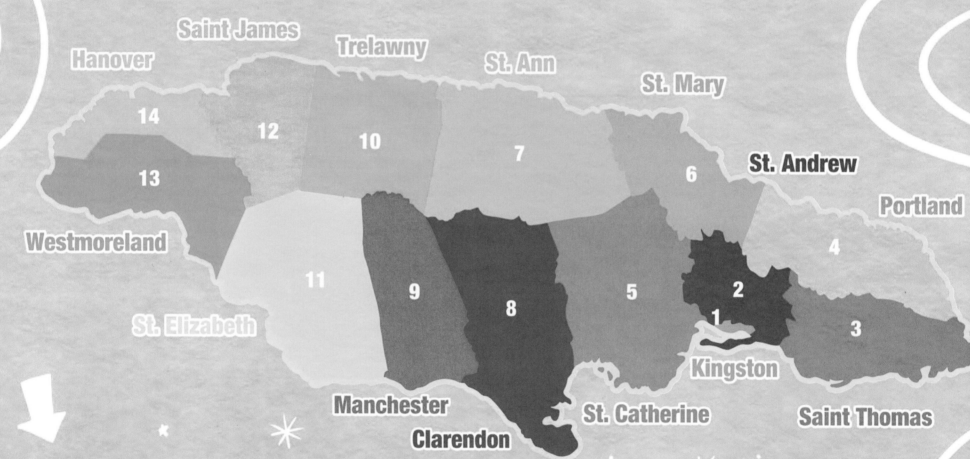

Saint James

Trelawny

St. Ann

St. Mary

Hanover

14

12

10

7

6

St. Andrew

13

Portland

Westmoreland

4

11

9

8

5

2

1

3

St. Elizabeth

Kingston

Manchester

St. Catherine

Saint Thomas

Clarendon

Jamaica is divided into 14 parishes.
The capital of Jamaica is Kingston, which is also the island's largest city.
I have a lot of family and friends who live in Kingston.
I also have a lot of family and friends in the parish of St. Catherine.

Personal Specimen

The official currency used in Jamaica is the Jamaican dollar. ($, J$, JA$). The U.S dollar is also accepted and used by many tourists.

Personal Specimen

What does the flag of Jamaica look like?

The colors of the Jamaican flag are black, green, and gold.

"The sun shineth, the land is green, and the people are strong and creative" is the symbolism of the colors of the flag.

What about the languages spoken in Jamaica?

English	Patois
Car	Cyar
Down	Dung
Friend	Fren
Give me	Gimme
In the	Inna di
Dog	Dawg

English is the official language of Jamaica. Although English is the official language of the country, Jamaican Patois is the most widely spoken. The Jamaican Patois is also referred to as Jamaican Creole or Patwa. Jamaican Patois is a form of English Creole developed on the island during the slave trade.

Are there any famous landmarks in Jamaica?

The Bob Marley Museum

Devon House

Dunn's River Falls

Rose Hall Great House

There are a lot of famous landmarks in Jamaica. Here are just a few.
The Bob Marley Museum, Devon House, Dunn's River Falls, and Rose Hall Great House.

What are some of the things for which Jamaica is famous ?

Some of the things Jamaica is well-known for are Reggae music, Bob Marley, Usain Bolt, the Jamaican Bobsled team, Blue Mountain coffee and a whole lot more!

What are some popular foods/dishes/cuisines in Jamaica?

Jamaica is well-known for a lot of delectable dishes! Here are a just few of them: Jerked chicken, curried goat, oxtails & beans, rice & peas, ackee & saltfish, escoveitch fish, festivals, fried plantains, saltfish fritters, black cake, sweet potato pudding, patties, gizzada, coconut drops, and sorrel.

Jerked Chicken

Curried Goat

Oxtails & Beans

....more foods/dishes/cuisines in Jamaica

Rice & Peas

Ackee & Saltfish

Escoveitch Fish

Fried Plantains

Festivals

Saltfish Fritters

27

....more foods/dishes/cuisines
in Jamaica

Black Cake

Sweet Potato Pudding

Patties

Gizzada

Coconut drops

Sorrel

I loved it there and will be visiting as often as I can.

Yum yum, good! Our tummies are now filled with all those yummy foods from Jamaica. Continuing our culture ride, we are now headed to North America. We will learn a little about the powerful U.S.A. Follow me as we explore some more...

U.S.A

Jamaica

Welcome to
The United States of America

U.S.A

Georgia

This is the country where my sister, Ari'el
and my older brother, Landon were born.
It is called The United States of America (U.S.A.).
They were both born in the State of Georgia.

Where is the United States of America Located?

The U.S.A. is in North America. The country is bordered on the west by the Pacific Ocean and to the east by the Atlantic Ocean. Along the northern border is Canada and the southern border is Mexico.

Canada

Pacific Ocean

United States of America

Atlantic Ocean

Mexico

How many states are there in the United States of America?

The U.S.A is divided into 50 States.
My older sister, Ariel and one of my older brothers, Landon were born in the State of Georgia. We currently live in this State. The capital of the U.S.A is Washington, D.C.

What is the official currency of the United States of America?

Personal Specimen

The official currency of The United States of America and its territories is the U.S. dollar. The U.S. dollar is the most common currency used by tourists.

Personal Specimen

What does the flag of the United States of America look like?

Red, white, and blue are the colors of the flag of the U.S.A.

It has 7 red stripes and 6 white ones.
These 13 stripes represent the original 13 colonies.
There are 50 stars which represent each State.

What about the languages spoken in the U.S.A?

> The official language in the United States is English. The top 10 languages in the U.S.A are: English, Spanish, Chinese, French & French Creole, Tagalog, Vietnamese, Korean, German, Arabic, Russian (According to bilingualkidspot.com)

English	One		**Vietnamese**	Mot
Spanish	Uno		**Korean**	Hana
Chinese	Yi	**Examples**	**German**	Eins
French	Un/Une		**Arabic**	Wahid
Tagalog	Isa		**Russian**	Odin

Are there any famous landmarks in the United States of America?

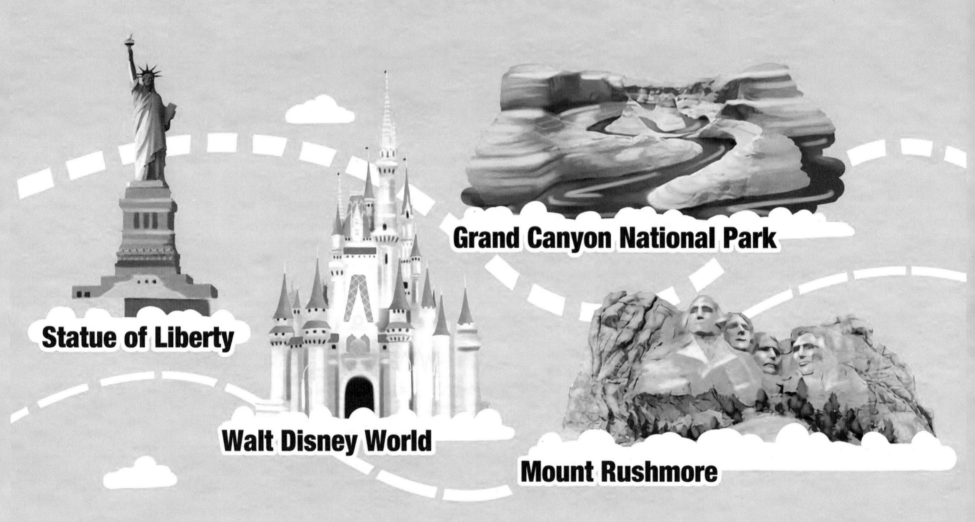

Statue of Liberty

Walt Disney World

Grand Canyon National Park

Mount Rushmore

Some famous landmarks in the United States are the Statue of Liberty, Walt Disney World, Grand Canyon National Park, and Mount Rushmore.

What are some of the things for which the United States of America is famous ?

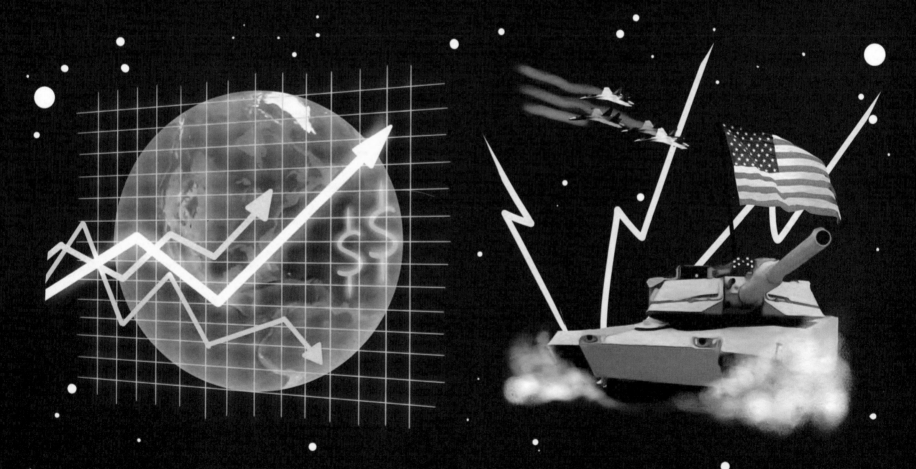

The United States is famous for having the world's most dominant economic and military power.

What popular foods/dishes/cuisines are in the United States of America?

Some popular foods/dishes/cuisines enjoyed in the U.S.A. are hamburgers, grits, drop biscuits and sausage gravy, ham hock and collard greens, Louisiana seafood boil, Philly cheesesteak, New York style calzones and pizzas, BBQ, mac & cheese, and more.

Grits

Ham hock & Collard Greens

Hamburgers

Drop Biscuits & Sausage Gravy

....more foods/dishes/cuisines in the United States of America

Louisiana Seafood Boil

New York Style Calzones

Philly Cheesesteak

New York Style Pizza

BBQ

Mac & Cheese

Which is your MOST favorite?

Let's practice some of the different languages from my cultures

English	Patwa	Arabic
What is your name?	Wah yu name?	Ma hu asmak?
How are you?	How yu du?	Kayf halikm?
How old are you?	Yu a oo much?	Kam eamruk?
Where do you live?	Weh yu live?	'Ayn taeish?
I'm going to school.	Mi a gu a school.	'Ana dhahib lilmudrasat.
The boys are eating.	Di bwoys dem a nyam.	Al'awlad yakuluna.

Thank You!

Thank you for walking through my 3 different cultures with me.
I hope you enjoyed this informational and fun journey.
If you have not yet visited any of these countries, you should.
You will have a great time! You will learn a whole lot more.
As I continue to learn about my backgrounds, I hope to learn
about other people's cultures too. We are different in several
ways, but we have a lot of similarities. Don't forget to love
yourself and love your backgrounds.

Reflection: What were some of the things you
enjoyed about this cultural journey?

A Few Clips of Me Enjoying My Cultures

At a Hawaiian themed brunch in Abu Dhabi

Loving my Jamaican style dress as I ate a treat while at a Farmer's market in my hometown GA, U.S.A

Eating patty from a Jamaican shop here in U.S.A.

Enjoying the manmade beach at Palm Island, Dubai

My dad and I enjoying ice-cream at the famous Devon House Ice-Cream shop in Jamaica.

Feasting on this tasty treat in my current hometown, GA.

Share and Discuss

1. Which of the landmarks mentioned in the story have you already visited or would like to visit?
2. What were some of your favorite foods mentioned? Did you see any new ones that you would like to try?
3. Which of these countries would you like to visit? Why?
4. Would you like to learn to speak any of the languages that were discussed in this book? If yes, which?
5. Have you ever traveled to another country? What was your experience like? What were some of the things that you did while there?
6. Are you able to locate all these 3 countries on a map or a globe?
7. What are 2 things you would share with a friend about your culture journey after reading this book?
8. Do you know a lot about where you are from? What are some of the things you would tell others about your culture(s)?

Lightning Source UK Ltd.
Milton Keynes UK
UKRC011123161220
375275UK00001B/4